THE VICTORIA AND ALBERT COLOUR BOOKS

FIRST PUBLISHED IN GREAT BRITAIN BY
WEBB & BOWER (PUBLISHERS) LIMITED
9 COLLETON CRESCENT, EXETER, DEVON EX2 4BY
AND MICHAEL JOSEPH LIMITED, 27 WRIGHTS LANE, LONDON W8 5TZ
IN ASSOCIATION WITH THE VICTORIA AND ALBERT MUSEUM, LONDON

COPYRIGHT © WEBB & BOWER (PUBLISHERS) LIMITED,
THE TRUSTEES OF THE VICTORIA AND ALBERT MUSEUM,
CARROLL, DEMPSEY & THIRKELL LIMITED 1988

BOOK, COVER AND SLIP CASE DESIGN BY CARROLL, DEMPSEY & THIRKELL LIMITED

BRITISH LIBRARY CATALOGUING IN PUBLICATION DATA

MENDES, VALERIE
NOVELTY FABRICS - (THE VICTORIA AND ALBERT COLOUR BOOKS)
1. TEXTILE FABRICS
I. TITLE II. SERIES
667'. 02864 TS1765

ISBN 0-86350-217-2

PRODUCTION BY FACER PUBLISHING
COLOUR REPRODUCTION BY PENINSULAR REPRO SERVICE, EXETER
TYPESET IN GREAT BRITAIN BY OPTIC

PRINTED AND BOUND IN HONG KONG BY
MANDARIN OFFSET

THE VICTORIA AND ALBERT COLOUR BOOKS

NOVELTY
FABRICS

INTRODUCTION BY
VALERIE MENDES

WEBB & BOWER
MICHAEL JOSEPH
MCMLXXXVIII

INTRODUCTION

THIS SELECTION of wittily conceived figurative designs and semi-representational patterns of inanimate objects were printed (mainly by roller) on lightweight fabrics between 1924 and 1946 as alternatives to more traditional textiles known as florals, geometrics and plains. Amusing, reasonably priced, mostly washable and sturdy, fun prints proved indispensable to the ever-expanding summer leisure wear industry and to the market for novelty yardage. Manufacturers sold these fanciful goods to fashion centres in Europe and America and a certain amount of cross-fertilisation of ideas and decorative themes is apparent. The vogue for nautical imagery became international as did humorous creations such as Felix the Cat who originated in America. Surviving samples in the Victoria and Albert Museum represent but a fraction of the designs that went into production and cannot give a completely even survey of the genre.

In 1925, Kneeland Green, Artistic Director of the Stehli Silks Corporation, New York introduced 'Americana Prints'. His article in *The Studio* (1929) outlined the venture which provided new dress fabrics for customers who were 'sick and tired of the conventional florals and polka dots which were 'created' by $25 a week copyists after a bicyle tour of Racinet's *L'Ornement Polychrome'*. By using talented American artists he achieved 'silk designs that tell a story' and reflected 'the modern American scene and temper'. Photographs of 'unconsidered trifles of everyday life' including mothballs and sugar lumps *(plate 3)* carpet tacks, buttons and thread were the starting points for Edward Steichen's designs which have a powerful three dimensional quality. A similar force is apparent in 'Pegs' *(plate 8)* where wooden pegs

7

are 'suspended' in sharp perspective against vivid red. Belonging to the same semi-abstract group, a smart blue and cream silk has toadstools scattered on a spotted background *(plate 14)*. In patriotic vein, the tennis star Helen Wills Moody ('Little Poker Face') reworked elements from the American flag into a meandering trellis in chic navy, red and cream *(plate 10)*. Drawing on her tennis experience she created a mauve and pink sequence of women players in action *(plate 17)*. Their low-waisted dresses and bandeaux evoke another famous 1920s champion – Suzanne Lenglen.

Stehli silks took pride in the dual nature of their prints featuring tiny stylised human figures. From a distance they appear to be geometric repeats while in close up they are miniature scenes from American daily life. Rows of boater-clad spectators in 'Stadium' *(plate 13)* were probably inspired by crowds at a baseball match. Press releases confirm that 'Rhapsody' *(plate 6)* was based upon Paul Whiteman's orchestra playing Gershwin's 'Rhapsody in Blue'. At a quick glance it seems to be an ordinary blue and white spotted silk but on scrutiny the carefully drawn jazz musicians come into focus. John Held Jr's droll patterns were used almost exclusively for informal clothes and accessories. One of his 1920s head squares depicting flappers and their cohorts golfing, cycling and playing tennis led to a number of costumes in Ken Russell's film *The Boyfriend*. Clayton Knight drew 'April' *(plate 11)* with its driving rain and rainbows while watching New York commuters one showery afternoon rushing towards the subway sheltering under umbrellas. Anita Loos's best seller *Gentlemen Prefer Blondes* prompted Ralph Barton's futuristic line pattern *(plate 12)*. Brunettes hang their heads despondently as top hatted suitors hasten away from them offering bouquets to a single blonde who confidently holds her pointed nose in the air.

In spite of the British textile trade's alarming decline between the wars surviving cotton printers retained their specialities and many included novelty ranges in their seasonal collections. Activities of the northern based industry were centred in the Calico Printers' Association (CPA) – a conglomerate with Manchester headquarters. Originally an amalgamation of forty-six printworks and thirteen merchant businesses the CPA was established in 1899 and said to encompass 85% of all British calico printing. Its protective aims were to boost trade and efficiency while eliminating rivalry. Throughout the 20th century, faced with the damaging effects of war, overwhelming foreign competition and other economic adversities the Association was compelled to reduce its operations drastically. In the 1970s it became English Calico and subsequently the Tootal Group, as it remains today. The printed rayon *(plates 31-2)* had its pattern registered by the CPA in October 1936. Registration deemed that the design was 'novel', assigned it a number (in chronological sequence) and copyrighted it for an initial five years. Like the earlier 'Americana Prints', 'Fun and Games' *(plates 31-2)* depicts mundane objects in this case the paraphernalia of drawing room games and parties – playing cards, skittles, bunting and paper streamers.

According to Pevsner's *An Enquiry into Industrial Art in England,* CUP, 1937, the textile industry was 'one of the largest users of designs in Britain' (a leading dress fabric manufacturer required 800 a year). Work of professional textile designers usually remained anonymous whereas designs by famous artists were acknowledged and much publicised. Mass producing dress fabrics by engraved roller printing has always been a financially risky business as the fashion market is notoriously fickle. Thousands of yards of a new design has to be sold to recoup costs.

Health cults, leisurely recreations and pursuit of the sun became fashionable in the late 1920s. By the mid-1930s adverisements for cruises and cruise wear editorials were ubiquitous. A new phenomenon, play clothes, emerged to meet these trends. Manufacturers developed cottons which proved technically and decoratively ideal for such styles. Innovations included pre-shrunk washable cottons with guaranteed fast colours, crease-resistant qualities and permanently glazed goods. Firms gave their inventions catchy names. Tootals washing cotton was christened 'Tobalcro', an uncrushable Moygashel linen became 'Spring Bak' while British Celanese introduced a non-wrinkle

'Cruising Crêpe' and 'Playtime Prints'. 'Wear more cotton than ever', demanded *Vogue* (June, 1937) and a 1938 Ferguson advertisement stated that 'cotton takes first place under the sun'. Brightly patterned cottons made practical yet attractive resort wear – playsuits, beach rompers and washable summer dresses called tub frocks. Fashion journalists employed a jocular tone when describing these 1930s fads with phrases like 'jolly holiday outfits', 'the merriest of prints' and 'cottons are gayer than they've ever been'.

In her Royal Society of Arts lecture 'Dress Fabrics' (December 1934), Alison Settle, the editor of *Vogue* made a point that textile manufacturers had to bear in mind 'the cruising influence with its strong seaside motifs of starfish and anchors, shells and coral'. Indeed printed fabrics sported a bewildering array of nautical images. Sailors were especially popular and in 1934 trios of jaunty matelots hornpiped across a vivid orange back cloth *(plate 9)*. Six years later sailors playing concertinas were incorporated into a more subdued vertical stripe *(plate 28)*. Cheerful red, white and blue was a much used holiday colour scheme. Blue bathing beauties of 1937 in white swim suits scud over a red sea on air beds *(plate 7)*. The tricolour was joined by yellow and black in a rather fussy pattern *(plate 26)* wherein ogees are quartered to enclose aquatic emblems. Simple yacht shapes printed on cotton piqué show the superiority of an uncluttered design approach and a limited palette *(plate 1)*. An unusual play print *(plate 15)* utilises sea horses, starfish and rope in a nauseous combination of yellows, green and black. Most extraordinary is a cotton decorated with menacing blue, magenta and yellow jelly fish drifting over seaweed fronds *(plate 27)*.

The semi-realistic portrayal of birds and animals has long been a main theme in the art of textile design. The awkwardly plump birds *(plate 29)* appear to have difficulty in maintaining flight yet make a sophisticated repeat. Sharing a weight problem but with sentimental appeal tubby penguins were screen printed on an Old Beach linen for nursery consumption in 1937 *(plate 2)*. Dilkusha of Berkley Square advertised that 'the smartest women of four great modern capitals are insistent in their praise of clothes created by Dilkusha'. They commissioned the precisely interlocked diagonal of horseheads *(plate 30)* for making up into leisure wear. In contrast to this emphatic equestrian design, fleeting race horses with tiny jockeys are freely drawn with minimal lines giving an evanescent quality to a post-war dress crêpe *(plate 24).*

Children's dress fabrics and nursery textiles were and remain prime targets for narrative scenes extracted from illustrated books and comics. Adults borrowed the idea of romper suits from infant fashions and made them in nursery fabrics to give them further light-hearted appeal. Pat Sullivan's sturdy little cartoon cat, Felix was a perfect character for textile patterning and provided fun for wearers of all ages. On a glazed cotton *(plate 22)* he befriends a mouse and they set off on travels together. Spotlit, Felix the musician *(plate 21)* entertains his young audience who listen on early wireless sets. 1920s 'beach culture' encompassed the whole family. Young, trendily clad, sausage-limbed adventurers in 1929 *(plate 18)* go crabbing, tumble into the sea and nearly drown their dollies.

With a predominantly blue and green colourway a dress crêpe printed in 1936 *(plate 23)* illustrates the decorative potential of architecture and topography. Its aerial countryside view has broken swirling movement formed by hillocks to which cling trees and cottages.

Dancers were choreographed in a multitude of lively textile designs. Diminutive pierrots and jesters cavort clutching balloons at their 1924 fancy dress party *(plate 4).* More pierrots are spreadeagled in a severely geometric manner to give the impression of acrobatic movement *(plate 5).* Images of a dancing peasant girl in festival costume dominate a furnishing print of 1938 *(plate 20).* Around her swirling skirts the designer has neatly fitted a village scene. Waltzing couples in formal evening dress of 1941 *(plate 25)* are practically obscured by immense balloons and streamers in primary colours. A number of British firms continued to make 'luxury' fabrics mainly for export though some found their way onto the home market) at the onset of World War II. When feasible they attempted to dispel the gloom with brilliantly coloured patterns. Later, under the Concentration of Industry Scheme many factories were closed and others turned over to the manufacture of war necessities including camouflage materials, gas mask discs and regimental badges. Printed dress fabrics played their part in Britain's victory campaign and designs with a message were issued to rouse patriotism and fighting instincts. Fougasse's 'Careless Talk Costs Lives' cartoons were roller printed onto dress weight cottons and rayons; Jacqmar issued a now famous series of propoganda scarves and yard-age with the 'Dig for Victory' slogan made utilitarian garments. After the Battle of Britain, the V for Victory sign became the central motif of a finely drawn, aggressive pattern with falling bombs and war planes *(cover)*. Meant for head scarves it has a border incorporating the morse code signal for victory.

Clothes rationing was introduced in June 1941. This restrictive system prompted 'Coupons' *(plate 19)*. Flattened out, miniscule garments (ranging from underclothes to evening gowns) drawn and coloured in a naive manner are arranged on a background littered with the number 66 (one year's clothing coupon allowance). By each stretched out item is noted the amount of coupons which had to be surrendered when that article was purchased.

Fun prints held great appeal for some couturiers, most notably for Elsa Schiaparelli. She appreciated fabrics which had that 'little bit extra' and when the market failed to provide them she worked with artists and manu-facturers to achieve her exact requirements. She understood the worth of visual jokes on textiles but most significantly translated them into witty yet sophisticated clothes. Early in her career she commissioned an innovative print of a newspaper cuttings collage (her own compilation) from the textile manufacturer Colcombet. Everyone thought that she was misguided but the textile quickly became a best seller. Vogue (March 1938) illustrated some typical Schiaparellis, among them a town ensemble with pink snails crawling over it, a playsuit printed with postage stamps and a day dress (from the 'Circus Collection') with clowns fooling on a pink crêpe ground. Later, the printed rayon 'Coupons' met her need for the unusual and she made it into a cocktail jacket and bag.

That designer of intricately cut clothes, Charles James, shared a similar desire for the extraordinary but unlike Schiaparelli he did not become involved with the development of special prints. He generally favoured sumptuous, plain materials but for a draped evening robe of 1938 he selected a viridian silk crêpe with a somewhat macabre pattern of flowing white masks and tiny stars designed and signed by Jean Cocteau *(plate 16)*. Considered to be merely part of holiday fun most of these amusing prints were made into short-lived summer clothes for play and relaxation. In this context their frivolities were both appropriate and acceptable. However, seen as marginal, their wit and ingenuity were given but passing acclaim. Thus it is fortunate that some examples, continual sources of delight, remain to document this ephemeral development of 20th century textiles.

All works illustrated are printed dress fabrics (unless otherwise stated) from the Department of Textile, Furnishings and Dress, Victoria and Albert Museum. Photography by Richard Davis.

Cover 'Victory V', cotton, *Calico Printers' Association, English, 1941*. 1 'Yatch', cotton piqué, *Tootal Broadhurst Lee & Co., English, 1941*. 2 'Penguin', screen printed furnishing linen, *Old Bleach Linen Co., Northern Irish, 1936*. 3 'Mothballs and Sugar', Edward Steichen, crêpe de Chine, *Stehli Silks Corporation, American, 1927*. 4 'Fancy Dress', cotton, F. Steiner, *English, 1924*. 5 'Pierrot', cotton, *Calico Printers' Association, English, 1937*. 6 'Rhapsody', John Held Jr., crêpe de Chine, *Stehli Silks Corporation, American, 1927*. 7 'Surfers', cotton, *Calico Printers' Association, English, 1937*. 8 'Pegs', Charles B. Falls, crêpe de Chine, *Stehli Silks Corporation, American, 1927*. 9 'Matelot' cotton, *Calico Printers' Association, English, 1934*. 10 'Stars and Stripes', Helen Wills Moody, crêpe de Chine, *Stehli Silks Corporation, American, 1927*. 11 'April', Clayton Knight, crêpe de Chine, *Stehli Silks Corporation, American, 1927*. 12 'Gentlemen Prefer Blondes', Ralph Barton, crêpe de Chine, *Stehli Silks Coporation, American, 1927*. 13 'Stadium', René Clarke, crêpe de Chine, *Stehli Silks Coporation, American, 1927*. 14 'Toadstools', crêpe de Chine, *Stehli Silks Corporation, American, 1927*. 15 'Sea Horses', cotton, *Calico Printers' Association, English, 1938*. 16 'Masks', Jean Cocteau, silk crêpe, *French, 1938*. 17 'A Game of Tennis', Helen Wills Moody, crêpe de Chine, *Stehli Silks Coporation, American, 1927*. 18 'Seaside', furnishing cotton, *Calico Printers' Association, English, 1929*. 19 'Coupons', rayon crêpe, *Calico Printers' Association, English, 1941*. 20 'Festival', furnishing cotton, *Tootal Broadhurst Lee & Co, English, 1938*. 21 'Musical Felix', after Pat Sullivan, cotton, *Calico Printers' Association, English, 1924*. 22 'Felix and the Mouse', after Pat Sullivan, cotton, *Calico Printers' Association, English, 1924*. 23 'Aerial View', rayon crêpe, *Calico Printers' Association, English, 1936*. 24 'Jockeys', rayon crêpe, *Calico Printers' Association, English, 1945*. 25 'Last Waltz', cotton, *Tootal Broadhurst Lee & Co, English, 1942*. 26 'Nautical', cotton, *Calico Printers' Association, English, 1940*. 27 'Jelly Fish', cotton, *Calico Printers' Association, English, 1945*. 28 'Sea Shanties', cotton, *Calico Printers' Association, English, 1940*. 29 'Doves', screen printed cotton furnishing, *Calico Printers' Association, English, 1935*. 30 'Horsehead', cotton, *Dilkusha Ltd, English, 1936*. 31-32 'Fun and Games', rayon crêpe, *Calico Printers' Association, English, 1936*.

Plates 3, 6, 8, 10-17 given by the Stehli Silks Corporation. Cover, Plates 1, 4, 5, 7, 9, 15, 18-32 given by the Manchester Design Registry. Plate 16 given by Mr Charles James.

THE PLATES

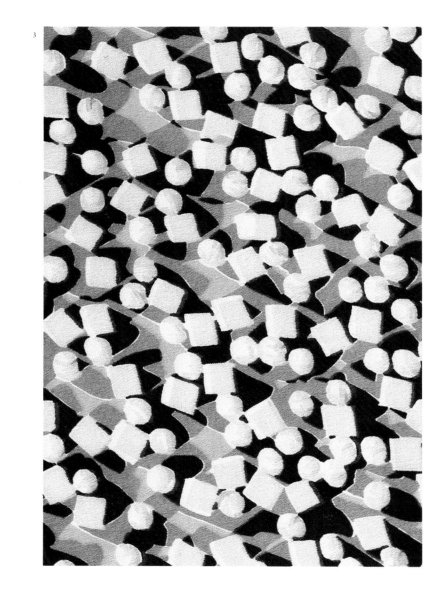

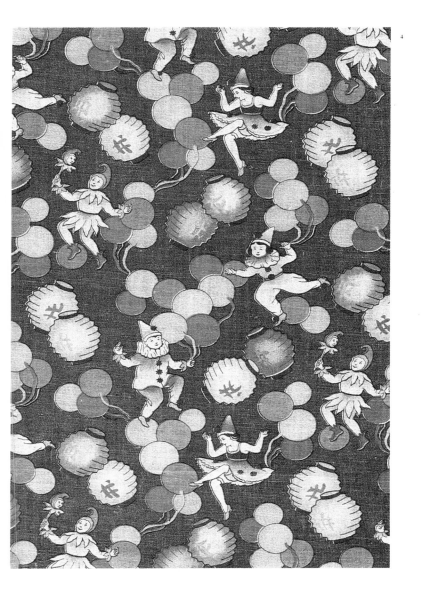

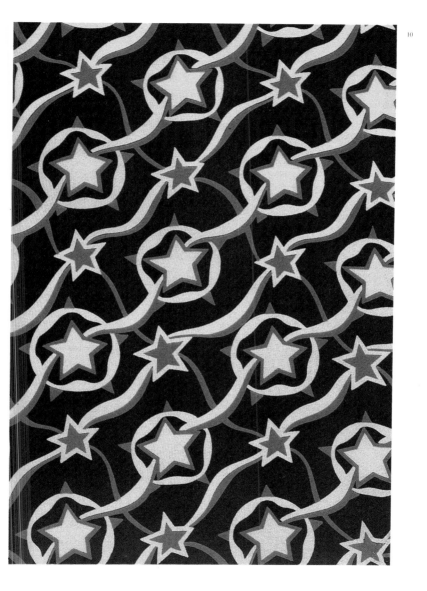

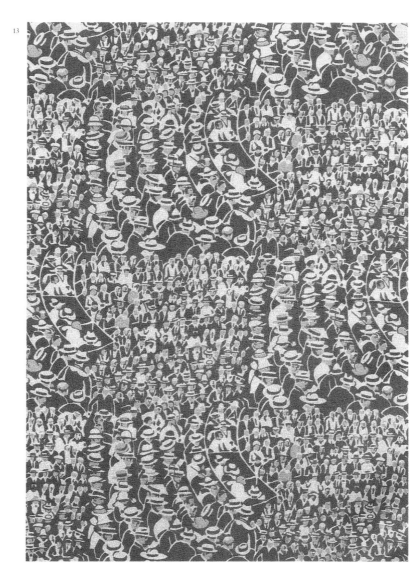

21

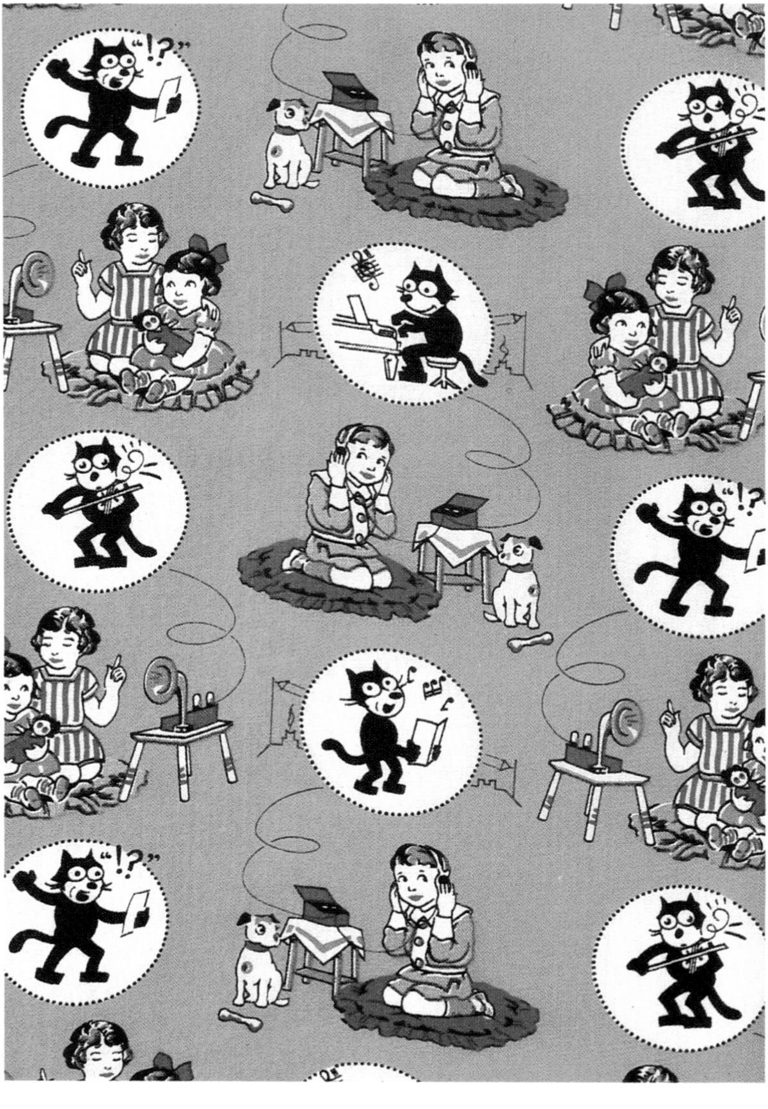

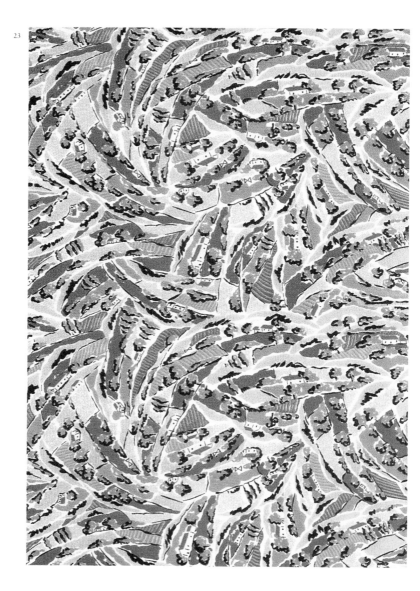

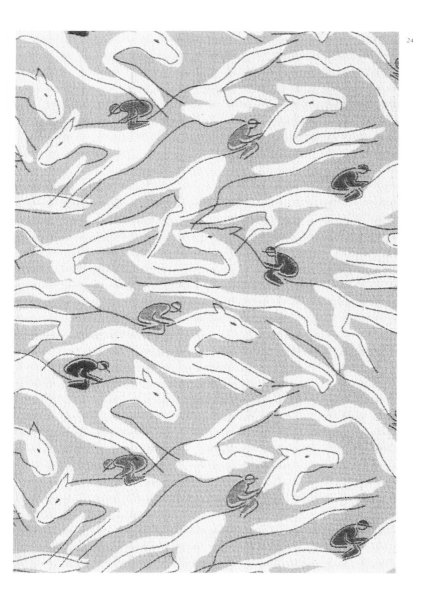

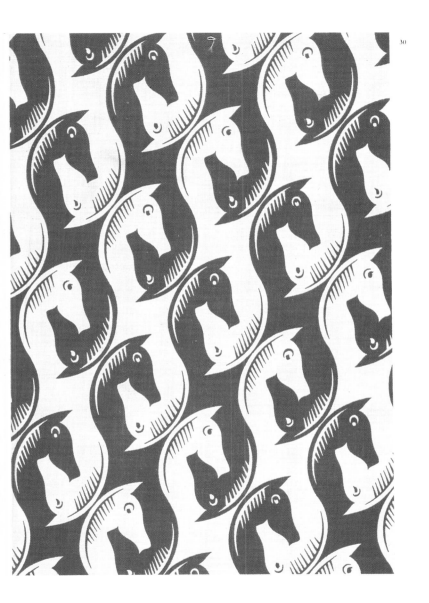

THE
VICTORIA
& ALBERT
COLOUR
BOOKS

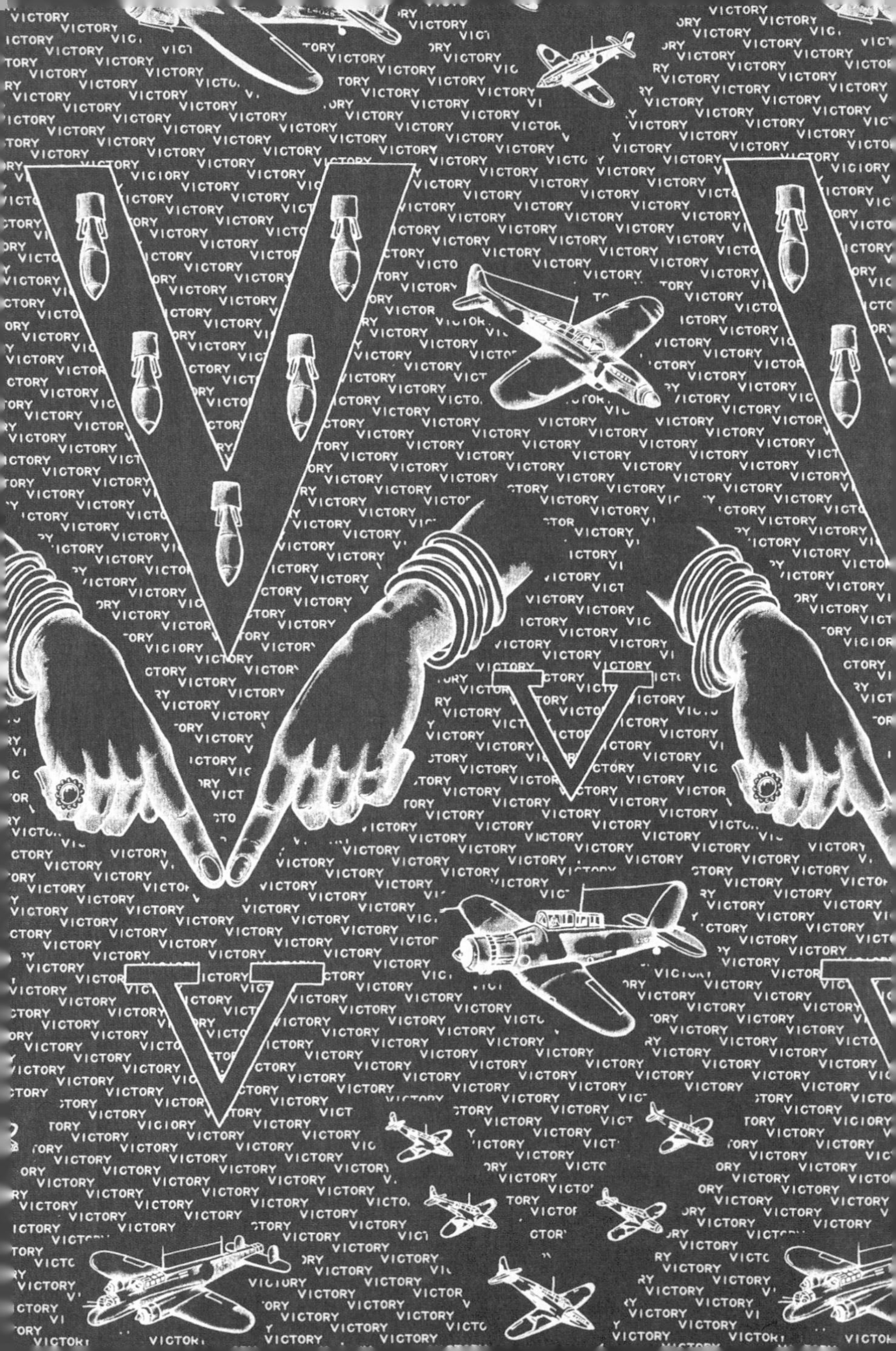
VICTORY